NATURE ALL YEAR LONG

CLARE WALKER LESLIE

Greenwillow Books, New York

ACKNOWLEDGMENTS

Grateful acknowledgments go to my family, who understand my need to do books; to Chuck Roth, Senior Research/Development Associate at Education Development Center of Newton, Massachusetts, who carefully oversaw scientific accuracy; to the staff at Massachusetts Audubon Society, who tirelessly answered questions; and to the editors at Greenwillow, who believed in this book from the beginning.

Colored pencils, pen-and-ink, and watercolors were used for the full-color art.
The text type is ITC Galliard.
Copyright © 1991 by Clare Walker Leslie
All rights reserved. No part of this book may be reproduced or utilized in any form or by any means, electronic or mechanical, including photocopying, recording, or by any information storage and retrieval system, without permission in writing from the Publisher, Greenwillow Books, a division of William Morrow & Company, Inc., 1350 Avenue of the Americas, New York, NY 10019.
Printed in Singapore by Tien Wah Press
First Edition   10 9 8 7 6 5 4 3 2 1

Library of Congress Cataloging-in-Publication Data

Leslie, Clare Walker.
Nature all year long / by Clare Walker Leslie.
    p.   cm.
Includes index.
Summary: Describes the different plants, animals, and landscapes that can be seen outdoors each month of the year.
ISBN 0-688-09183-0
1. Nature study—Juvenile literature.
2. Natural history—Outdoor books—Juvenile literature.
[1. Nature study.   2. Months.]
I. Title.   QH51.L47 1991
508—dc20   90-47866   CIP   AC

To my son, Eric,

whose love of nature

encouraged me to do this book

Introduction

In the world of nature, every month is slightly different from the next, and so is every season. But interestingly, what makes each month unique does not vary that much, year after year. Wherever you live, you can learn to notice these small changes in the landscape around you. Studying nature can be as interesting as a treasure hunt, full of discovery, adventure, and unexpected events.

This book is intended to give you ideas about what can be seen outdoors each month of the year. Wherever you live, whether in the country, city, or suburbs, in the woods, mountains, or desert, you can find interesting things to observe. The area described in this book is New England. Compare it with where you live and find the similarities and the differences. Choose the animals, plants, and landscapes you want to watch.

As you discover more about nature, you may find that some of your questions cannot be answered or that the answers keep changing. This is because scientists are still searching for the reasons behind some of the most common occurrences of life on earth. Much is still being learned about things like animal hibernation, bird migration, plant reproduction, and even the seasons themselves.

Keep a monthly calendar and regularly enter lists or drawings of what you see happening outdoors. Your class might work on a project to observe nature around the schoolyard throughout the year. Use the monthly FACTS column, the projects, and the information offered here as a guide.

The bibliography at the end of the book suggests some specific and general guides and references for nature study. Any library or bookstore should be able to help you find the books you need. Visit a local nature center and perhaps take part in some classes or field trips.

Watching what happens in nature through the year can make you more aware of how important it is to protect our natural landscape and all its inhabitants from destruction or misuse. It can also be a wonderful way to spend time outdoors alone, with a friend, or with your family. Learning about nature is an adventure that costs little money, needs little equipment or skill, and provides many hours of mystery, discovery, and fun.

FROST LINE

Animals That Sleep Through the Winter

What happens to animals in the winter? Many remain active, but many find a warm shelter and sleep away the cold months. If there is snow, it acts as insulation and keeps the ground underneath warmer than the air above.

In regions where it gets very cold, the ground freezes down to a varied depth called the FROST LINE. Some animals can survive in the frozen soil. But many must dig down below the frost line so their bodies will not freeze.

If an animal goes into so deep a sleep that its heartbeat and its breathing slow down and its body temperature drops, scientists call this HIBERNATION. Hibernating animals live off their own stored energy and do not wake until spring.
How do you think the animals in your neighborhood survive the winter?

1. A **cecropia moth** pupa lies resting within its cocoon, which the caterpillar spun around itself at summer's end before changing into a pupa.

2. A **woollybear caterpillar** hibernates before turning into an Isabella moth in the spring.

3. **Spotted salamanders** (newts) curl up under leaf piles, logs, or stone walls and become inactive.

4. Of the summer **bumblebee** colony, only the queen survives to live through the winter, hibernating in a hole under leaves. Since bumblebees are cold-blooded animals, they can survive partially frozen.

5. **Wood frogs** hibernate under stones, logs, or dried leaves. Also cold-blooded animals, they too can survive partially frozen.

6. **Woodchucks** (groundhogs) hibernate, snoozing the entire winter away in burrows they dug into the ground in early fall.

7. **Chipmunks** are light hibernators, waking occasionally to eat stored food or to poke above ground on warm days.

8. **Earthworms** hibernate 3'–6' down in the soil, where they cannot freeze.

9. **Voles** (meadow mice) remain active all winter, making tunnels in snow, grasses, or just below the soil.

Animals That Stay Active Through the Winter

During the cold months, those animals that do not die, sleep, or leave for a warmer climate must remain active. Animals that stay active put on extra layers of fat and grow thicker coats. Generally, they sleep during the day and are out hunting food at night. Winter is a good time to learn which animals stay active in your neighborhood, for you can often find their tracks in snow or mud.

Take out a sketch pad and draw the tracks you find. Identify them, using a guide to animal tracks.

JANUARY FACTS

■ January can be the coldest and harshest month for animals and plants. It is mating season for raccoons, foxes, owls, and gray squirrels.

■ The winter months provide an important time of rest and germination for a number of plants and animals.

■ The January full moon has been called the Hunger Moon by some native American tribes.

■ Since December 21, the days have been getting longer. By the end of the month, there will be almost 50 more minutes of daylight than at the end of December.

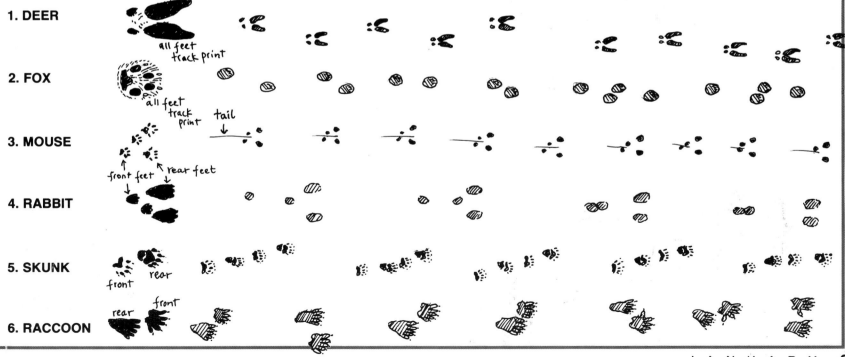

1. DEER
2. FOX
3. MOUSE
4. RABBIT
5. SKUNK
6. RACCOON

Birds That Stay North During the Winter

Depending on where you live, its climate and food sources, certain species of birds will remain year-round. Others will leave when fall comes, and some will move in from farther north for winter. You can have fun getting to know your local birds. Put out food to see what birds you can attract near you. Use a bird field guide and binoculars to help in identification.

Do any of these birds live in your neighborhood in winter?

1. chickadee
2. cardinal
3. pigeon
4. starling
5. goldfinch
6. downy woodpecker
7. blue jay
8. house sparrow

See which foods different birds prefer. Put out a feeder or scatter some birdseed on the ground.

Try putting out:
  sunflower seeds
  cracked corn
  suet
  thistle seed
  mixed seed
  stale bread.

You can buy bags of seed at a hardware store, supermarket, or local nature center.

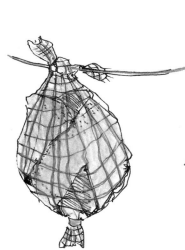

Plastic Jug Feeders
Find a milk, juice, or bleach jug. Cut out 3 or 4 3-sided windows, about 1½" × 1". Fill the jug with sunflower seeds and hang it on a porch or tree.

Suet Chunks
You can buy suet (meat fat) in food markets. Hang some in an old onion bag or in chicken wire mesh for woodpeckers and nuthatches to eat.

February 4—10

chickadee — ∥∥
blue jay — ∥∥
junco — ∥
cardinal — ∣
purple finch — ∥∣
crow — ∥
goldfinch — ∣

33 Oak St.

Snow — Mon + Tues.
Cloudy — Wed.
Sunny — Thurs + Fri
rain — Sat + Sun.

Keep a weekly list of birds you see at your feeder or around your neighborhood. Weather can affect the number and variety you see.

Using a needle and thread, make a long string of cranberries and popcorn. Birds, as well as squirrels and mice, like this food.

You Can Have a Winter Garden Indoors

Many florist shops and even supermarkets sell little pots of bulbs this time of year. Place the pots on a sunny windowsill or table, water the bulbs every few days, and watch them grow and flower. Draw the plants in their stages of growth. You can also buy loose bulbs from a garden mart and plant them yourself in soil or stones in a flowerpot or shallow bowl. Follow the directions given by the garden center.

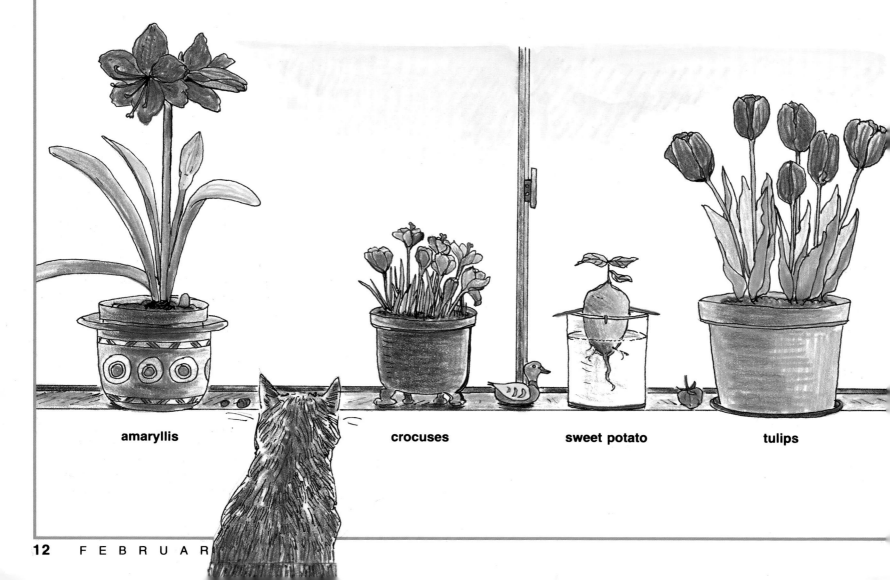

amaryllis   crocuses   sweet potato   tulips

What Are Bulbs, Tubers, and Corms?

Bulbs, tubers, and corms are all underground, reproductive stems that store food for next year's plants. In bulbs like amaryllis, tulip, or onion, the food is stored in fleshy scales surrounding a short, thin stem. In tubers like potatoes and carrots, the food is stored in the stem itself, which is thickened and spongy. A corm is a short, solid, underground stem, much like a tuber. It is often confused with a bulb. Crocuses and gladioli are corms.

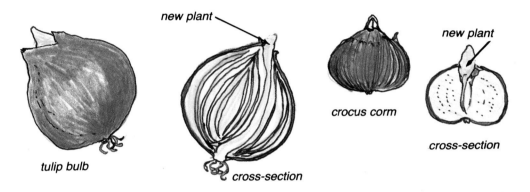

new plant

tulip bulb

cross-section

crocus corm

new plant

cross-section

What Are Seeds?

Seeds contain the new plant and are produced within the flower of the parent plant. Each seed grows only 1 plant. Beans are seeds. Wrap 3 beans in a damp paper towel and watch them sprout.

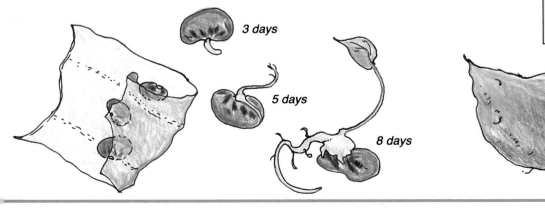

3 days

5 days

8 days

You can set a sweet potato, supported by toothpicks, in a glass of water, and it will soon grow roots and leaves. You can do the same with a carrot or a turnip.

Tapping Sugar Maple Trees for Syrup

sugar maple

Signs of Spring Outdoors

1. Some birds that have wintered in more southern states, such as robins and red-winged blackbirds, begin returning north.

2. The sap in sugar maple trees begins to flow. In certain states, people gather it to make maple syrup.

3. Early spring flowers, including snowdrops and crocuses, now bloom.

4. The woollybear caterpillar is still asleep.

5. On warm days, chipmunks may awaken for a while from their winter sleep and come out of their holes.

6. Roads and fields become muddy as ice and snow melt.

7. The cecropia moth still sleeps as a pupa inside its cocoon.

In late winter, a tree's sap begins flowing up through the trunk's veins from the roots, where it remained unfrozen all winter. (Sap is a watery liquid "food" produced within the tree's vessel system.) The returning sap feeds the tree's swelling buds, which soon will open into leaves.

The sap in sugar maples has a higher sugar content than that in other trees. Long ago, native Americans discovered it could be collected and boiled down to form a rich, sugary syrup for eating. 2 or 3 small tubes inserted 1″–2″ into a tree can divert some of the sap into hanging buckets without harming the tree. It takes almost 40 gallons of sap to make 1 gallon of syrup.

Different Tree Bud Shapes

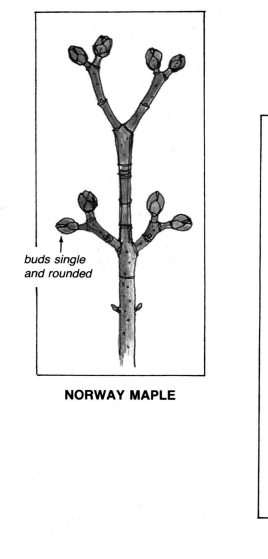

buds single
and rounded

NORWAY MAPLE

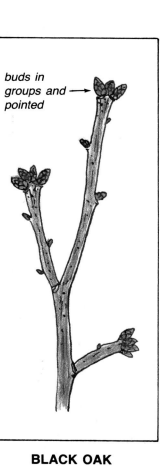

buds in
groups and
pointed

BLACK OAK

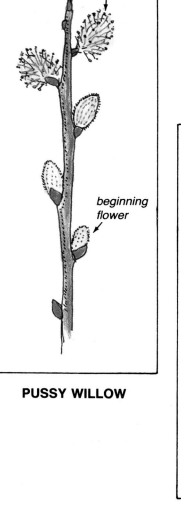

flowers

beginning
flower

PUSSY WILLOW

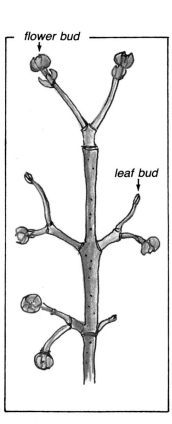

flower bud

leaf bud

**FLOWERING
DOGWOOD**

How to Identify Winter Twigs

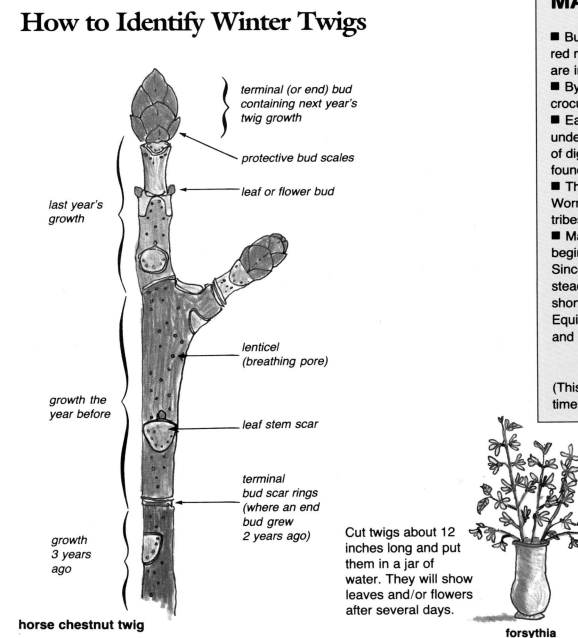

terminal (or end) bud containing next year's twig growth

protective bud scales

leaf or flower bud

last year's growth

lenticel (breathing pore)

growth the year before

leaf stem scar

terminal bud scar rings (where an end bud grew 2 years ago)

growth 3 years ago

horse chestnut twig

Cut twigs about 12 inches long and put them in a jar of water. They will show leaves and/or flowers after several days.

forsythia

Try: forsythia lilac apple cherry dogwood maple.

By bringing these twigs indoors where it is warm, you are just speeding up the natural process that takes place more slowly outdoors.

MARCH FACTS

■ Buds on trees begin to swell. Silver and red maple, pussy willow, poplar, and elm are in flower.

■ By the end of the month, snowdrops, crocuses, and early daffodils are in bloom.

■ Earthworms come up to the surface from underground. Worm castings (small piles of digested and excreted earth) can be found on lawns and in schoolyards.

■ The March full moon has been called the Worm Moon by some native American tribes.

■ March 21, the First Day of Spring, begins the second season of the year. Since December 21, the days have steadily been getting longer and the nights shorter. It is also called the Spring Equinox, for on this day the lengths of day and night are nearly equal.

Sunrise—around 5:45 A.M.

Sunset—around 5:57 P.M.

(This is Boston time. Check your area's times.)

Animals Now Come Out of Their Winter Sleep

1. Squirrels prepare nests, using masses of leaves stuffed into forks of tree branches.

2. Chipmunks leave their holes, looking for food and mates.

3. Male frogs, of species such as spring peepers, call from damp woods and ponds in search of mates.

4. In wet places, pussy willows bloom.

5. Spotted salamanders look for mates.

6. Earthworms, ants, sowbugs, and other small creatures emerge from deep in the soil or from under leaves and rocks, making good meals for robins and other animals.

7. Woodchucks come out of their burrows, looking for food and mates.

8. By early April, wood frogs have left their winter shelters for nearby ponds, where they find mates.

9. The cecropia moth pupa will sleep until the weather gets warm enough for it to transform into a butterfly and hatch out of its cocoon.

10. Bumblebee queens are ready to build nests and start new colonies in holes in the ground or in logs.

11. Woollybear caterpillars have spun cocoons around themselves.

12. Some old leaves still remain from last fall.

Stages of Life Changes for Certain Insects (Called Complete Metamorphosis)

1. EGG: Eggs are laid by an adult female.
2. LARVA: The larva hatches from an egg and is called a caterpillar, worm, maggot, or grub, depending on the species of insect.
3. PUPA: During this stage, the insect changes from a larva to an adult while wrapped inside a case called a pupa, cocoon, or chrysalis.
4. ADULT: This is the final and egg-laying stage for all insect species.

Changes in the Life of a Woollybear Caterpillar

During the summer, a female moth lays eggs on a leaf. After several weeks, small caterpillars hatch out of the eggs and grow bigger over the summer by eating leaves. They spend the winter in this stage.

1/16″ eggs

2½″

In the spring, each caterpillar spins a cocoon around itself and changes into a pupa, making the cocoon from its own body silk and hairs. In late spring, the pupa is transformed and breaks out of its cocoon as an adult Isabella moth.

1″

2″ wings

What changes in nature do you see happening around you?

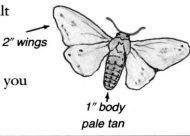

1″ body
pale tan

Water Is Necessary for All Life

All animals and plants need water to grow. More than half the earth's surface is covered by water. Every day, water evaporates into the air from plants, rivers, lakes, and seas. When the water vapor cools enough in some parts of the sky, it can condense to form a cloud. When the water droplets making up the cloud become large enough, they will fall as rain, sleet, or snow, depending on how cold the air is. In April, rain can make the land and all its newly growing plants seem to turn green overnight.

What Do Animals Do When It Rains?

Some birds huddle under eaves of buildings or within thickets of trees and shrubs. Other birds brave it out, ruffling up feathers to keep warmth in and rain out.

Spiders go to the edges of their webs, away from wet droplets that gather in the centers of the sagging webs.

Squirrels pull their tails over their heads, like umbrellas.

Small animals hide under leaf cover or in holes.

Large animals find protection under trees or turn against the wind and wait out the rain.

RAIN PROJECTS

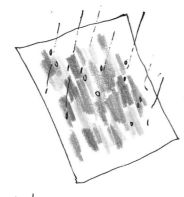

Using colored chalk, cover a piece of paper with chalk powder. Put the paper out in the rain and watch how raindrops make patterns on the chalk.

Put out a cup. See how much rain it collects in an hour, a day, or over several days.

Look to see how rain collects on leaves and flowers.

Go outdoors to see how rain travels along streets, settles in lawns, collects on leaves, or makes puddles in muddy yards. Listen to the sounds of rain. What are the smells of rain?

Spring Flowers

In a number of countries, May 1 is celebrated as a festival of spring. Some schools or towns have Maypole dances and games outdoors. Children make May baskets and garlands and give away bouquets of flowers. What flowers are coming into bloom around you? Can you find flowers in the woods, fields, or gardens where you live? Can you find flowers on trees and shrubs? A local guide to flowers will help you learn what flowers bloom in your area, and when.

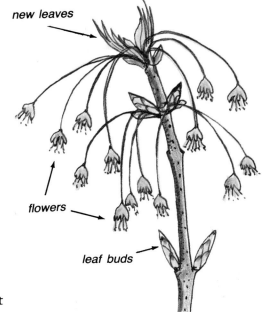

new leaves

flowers

leaf buds

sugar maple

Wildflowers

Wildflowers are those flowers that grow naturally in uncultivated places. Many have showy flowers and specialized growing needs. If picked, they may not grow again.

1. trout lily
2. lady's slipper
3. jack-in-the-pulpit

Weeds

Wildflowers are often called weeds when they grow out of place, as in someone's garden or lawn. Weeds grow easily, spread fast, and usually have tiny flowers that are not showy.

4. clover
5. poison ivy
6. dandelion

Garden Flowers

Garden flowers are flowers that have been planted and cared for in garden beds. Some must be replanted every year. These are called annuals. Some come up again and again and are called perennials.

7. tulips
8. pansies
9. marigolds

Tree Flowers

Some trees, like the apple and magnolia, have showy flowers. But most have small, less colorful flowers, like the sugar maple, whose flowers appear before the leaves emerge.

Some Types of Birds' Nests

Birds make a variety of nests, according to their species and where they live. Some make nests on rocky seacoasts, some in tree holes, some on the ground, and some on tree branches.

Try making a nest out of twigs, grasses, and bits of wool or cloth. Which bird's nest does yours most resemble?

The downy woodpecker builds a nest in a tree hole. It digs down 8"–10" and lays 3–6 shiny white eggs among a layer of wood chips.

The broad-winged hawk either makes a rough nest of sticks and old leaves, lining it with smaller twigs and bark, or uses a nest that was abandoned by a crow, squirrel, or another hawk. The female lays 2–3 eggs that are creamy white with dark streaks.

The northern oriole weaves a long basket using plant fibers, bark strips, and even scraps of wool, string, or fabric. The 4 or 5 eggs are beige with brown streaks.

Killdeer nest on the open ground, often in fields, gravel areas, or lawns. The nest depression is unlined or lined only with pebbles, grass, or woodchips. There are usually 4 eggs, tan with dark markings that make a perfect camouflage.

Sketching Birds

Take a sketch pad and pencil along when you are watching birds. Keep your drawings simple and don't worry about whether they are good or not. You will get better as you practice and learn more about how birds are shaped. Use a bird book to identify individual birds. There are different groups of birds—such as hawks, owls, ducks, song birds, herons, gulls—and different kinds of birds in each group—for example, broad-winged hawks or red-shouldered hawks.

MAY FACTS

■ May is one of the busiest months outdoors. Returning birds, blooming flowers, emerging insects, and days of sun and rain all keep both professional naturalists and anyone who likes to study nature busy outdoors.
■ Many fish, frogs, toads, salamanders, mosquitoes, and blackflies are laying eggs near and in freshwater places.
■ Many trees and shrubs are leafing out now.
■ The May full moon has been called the Full Flower Moon by some native American tribes.

BASIC SKELETON

A bird's shape can be drawn by making a circle for the head and an oval for the body, with tail, wings, bill, and legs added.

slight eye ring

blue / gray back + head

yellow

orange necklace

yellow

2 wing bars

♂ (male) parula warbler in sugar maple Mt. Auburn Cemetery 5/12 8:30 am

Now the Young of Birds and Animals Can Be Seen

Raccoons, voles, woodchucks, chipmunks, and deer, though born in April or May, make their first appearances outside their birthplaces in June. If water temperature has been warm enough, spotted salamanders will now be hatching from their eggs. If the queen bumblebee has set up her new hive, young bees may be out gathering food.

Since June has the most hours of daylight, animal and plant growth is at its peak. For many animals, the season of birth and growth is really very short, generally lasting only 3 or 4 months. By summer's end, most babies have become adults and leave their parents to survive on their own.

1. robins
2. raccoons
3. squirrels
4. voles (meadow mice)
5. spotted salamanders
6. woodchucks
7. A cecropia moth has hatched from its pupal cocoon.
8. deer
9. An Isabella moth has hatched from its pupal cocoon.
10. chipmunks
11. In June, the sun makes its highest arc through the sky.

Join a nature center this summer. Take a camping trip. Subscribe to a nature magazine. Go for walks outdoors as often as you can. Learn what the animals that live near you are doing.

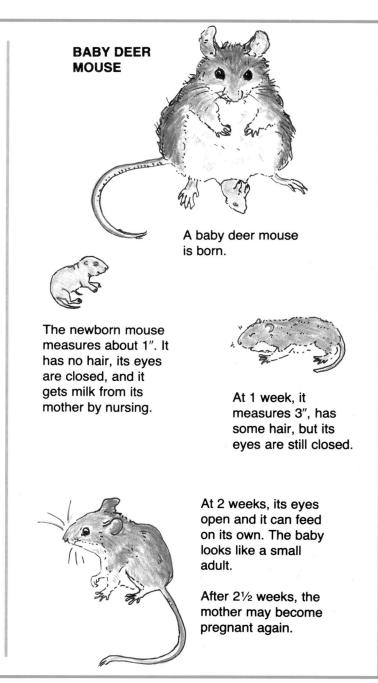

BABY DEER MOUSE

A baby deer mouse is born.

The newborn mouse measures about 1". It has no hair, its eyes are closed, and it gets milk from its mother by nursing.

At 1 week, it measures 3", has some hair, but its eyes are still closed.

At 2 weeks, its eyes open and it can feed on its own. The baby looks like a small adult.

After 2½ weeks, the mother may become pregnant again.

Summer Insects

In June, many insects hatch. Most are not harmful to people and, in fact, can be very useful. They are an important food for a variety of animals during the summer months.

On a warm night, turn on your porch light. Tape a white cloth below it.

See what insects are attracted to the light, hang on to the cloth, or climb on your screened door. (Because many insects are oriented to light, they can confuse a bright light with moonlight.) Some night-flying insects will stay long enough for you to get close so that you can observe and even draw them. Remember, insects are usually more afraid of you than you are of them.

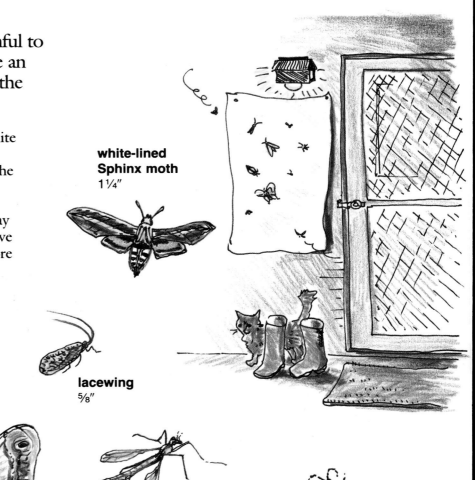

white-lined Sphinx moth
1¼"

firefly
⅝"

lacewing
⅝"

June beetle
1"

cecropia moth
3½"

crane fly
1½"

elderberry longhorn beetle
1"

ANATOMY OF AN INSECT

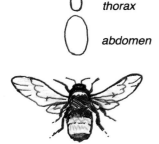

O head

O thorax

○ abdomen

All creatures having 3 body parts and 6 legs attached to the middle section, or thorax, are classified as insects. Most insects have 1 or 2 pairs of wings, also attached to the thorax.

A spider is not an insect. It has 2 body parts and 8 legs and is in the Class Arachnida.

Make simple line drawings of the insects that are attracted to your porch light. You may be surprised by the variety. Identify and label your drawings, using a field guide to insects.

June 28
Granville
9:30 pm
82°
hot, muggy
half moon
occasional
frog + bird song

2"
tan

Sphinx Moth
Pink

3/4"

all white body/ wings
fall webworm moth?

pale tan

3/8"

red + blue
leaf hopper

Crane fly

1"

JUNE FACTS

■ Evenings are long, providing more time to watch the sun set and shadows appear, and to listen to the choruses of birds, frogs, and insects.

■ The June full moon has been called the Hot Moon by some native American tribes.

■ June 21, the First Day of Summer, begins the third season of the year. It is the longest day of the year, when the earth in the Northern Hemisphere is tilted closest to the sun. It is also called the Summer Solstice because this is the time when the sun at midday reaches its highest position of the year. After this, the sun will gradually lower its path across the sky and the days will shorten as the earth tilts slowly away from the sun, heading once more toward winter.

> Sunrise—around 5:07 A.M.
> Sunset—around 8:25 P.M.

(This is Boston time. Check your area's times.)

■ The holiday of Midsummer's Eve and Midsummer's Day has long been celebrated in Europe on June 23–24, at about the time of the longest day of the year. In the far northern countries where winters are long, dark, and cold, it is an especially favored holiday. The sun, the health of the land, and the arrival of summer are honored with all-night parties, bonfires, and merrymaking.

Life in a Freshwater Pond

In July, you may visit a pond, lake, stream, or river. Here are some plants and animals that you are likely to find in and around a freshwater pond. (Ponds in your area may have somewhat different creatures.)

1. common cattail (3′–9′)
2. red-winged blackbird nesting in cattails
3. pickeral weed (1′–4′)
4. arrow arum (2′–5′)
5. ten-spot dragonfly (2″)
6. nymph (immature stage of ten-spot dragonfly) (¾″)
7. blackwing damselfly (1⅓″)
8. red-spotted salamander (newt) (3″–4″)
9. water beetles (1″)
10. water strider (¾″)
11. green frog (3″) and polliwogs (¾″)
12. mallard ducks
13. muskrat
14. painted turtles (5″–6″)
15. bass (6″–18″)

Sit quietly by a stream or pond and watch the activity there. Make a list of what you see, using a guidebook to help you learn more about freshwater life.

If you want to have a closer look at a few water animals, collect them in a plastic bowl or wide-mouthed jar filled with water from the stream or pond where you found them.

If you keep frog or salamander eggs for a while to watch them hatch, take only a few from the cluster and keep them in water from the stream or pond where you found them. Be sure to add fresh water weekly from an unpolluted source. (Tap water usually is not good to use because of the chlorine and other chemicals in it.) When the eggs hatch, return the young salamanders or frogs to where you found the eggs and let them go free.

STAGES IN A WOOD FROG'S LIFE

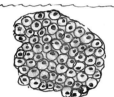

each egg about ⅛″

In early spring, egg masses are laid by a female wood frog in shallow freshwater places.

about ¾″

A tadpole hatches from each egg in 14–24 days.

Tadpole grows legs after about 2 weeks.

Tadpole begins developing lungs and losing tail.

frog about 1″

In early July, tadpole becomes adult frog and moves to land.

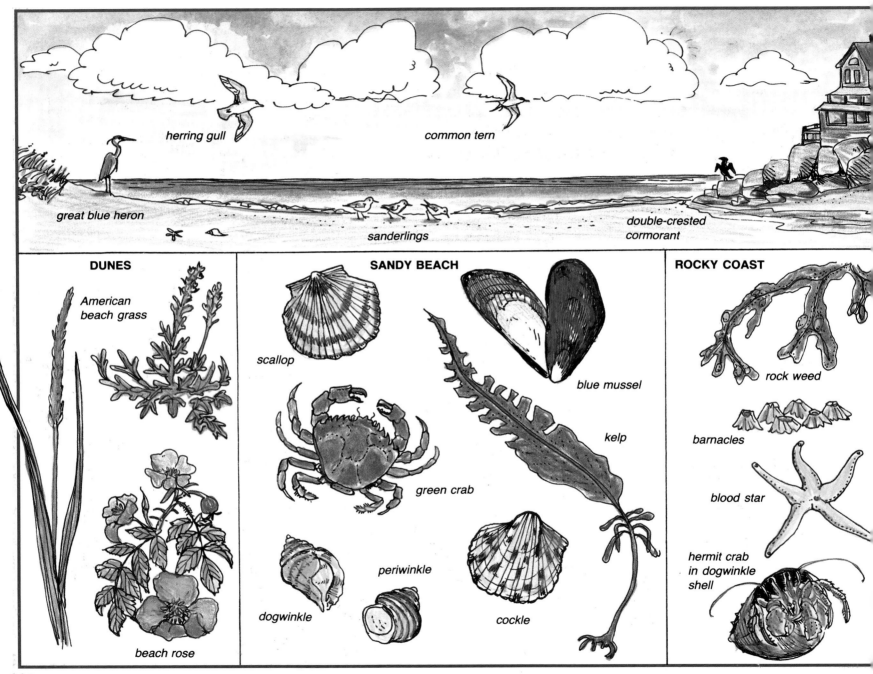

herring gull

common tern

great blue heron

sanderlings

double-crested cormorant

DUNES

American beach grass

beach rose

SANDY BEACH

scallop

blue mussel

green crab

kelp

dogwinkle

periwinkle

cockle

ROCKY COAST

rock weed

barnacles

blood star

hermit crab in dogwinkle shell

Life Along a Seacoast

If you visit the coast on a day in July, take along some buckets, shovels, collecting bags, a sketchbook, pencil, and a few guidebooks to seashore life. Collect seashells or empty crab shells. Glue them onto cardboard to make a collage, or create a hanging mobile using thread, all-purpose white glue, and driftwood.

A good way to learn why one habitat (a place where animals and plants live) is different from another is to study what creatures live there. How do freshwater and saltwater habitats differ?

JULY FACTS

- July is the height of the summer. Days are long and often hot. Big gatherings of clouds, called cumulus clouds or thunderheads, may bring storms with thunder, lightning, and rain.
- Plants are reaching their peak of growth in meadows, fields, and backyard lots.
- Bird choruses have quieted, for the adults are busy rearing young. Insects seem to be everywhere.
- By the end of July, daylight is almost 40 minutes shorter than just 1 month ago.
- The July full moon is sometimes called the Hay Moon because it gives farmers extra light to bring in the fresh-cut hay.

Meadows and Fields Are Filled with Activity

1. barn swallow
2. tiger swallowtail butterfly
3. 3 types of meadow grasses:
   a. orchard grass
   b. timothy
   c. redtop
4. yellowthroat warbler and young
5. meadow grasshopper
6. vole (meadow mouse)
7. caterpillar of cecropia moth
8. milkweed
9. adult monarch butterfly
10. field cricket
11. woodchucks
12. broad-winged hawk

Take a walk in a meadow, a backyard, or any open area. Listen for the rasping of grasshoppers, the pulsing of crickets, and the long buzz of cicadas. Do you hear any birds? See how many different flowers, insects, and grasses you can find. Take along a sketchbook and pencil or pen. Use this illustration as an example of one way to lay out a sketchbook page. Imagine what this place will look like in fall, winter, spring. Make drawings of how it will look in different seasons.

ANATOMY OF A FLOWER

pollen grains · stigma · anther · style · stamen (male part) · filament · pistil (female part) · sepal · ovules

August 6
North Hill
10:30 am
mid 70's
breezy. sunny
fields browning
over but still
lush
hear =
din of grasshoppers
song sparrow
wind in leaves
blue jay

Crab spider on milkweed leaf. Waiting for prey. Has no web! Changes color to suit surroundings

I 1/2"

broad-winged hawk circles over meadow. "ke-keeeer" call

rabbit droppings on deer path - where's rabbit now ??

I 1/4"

Common buttercup

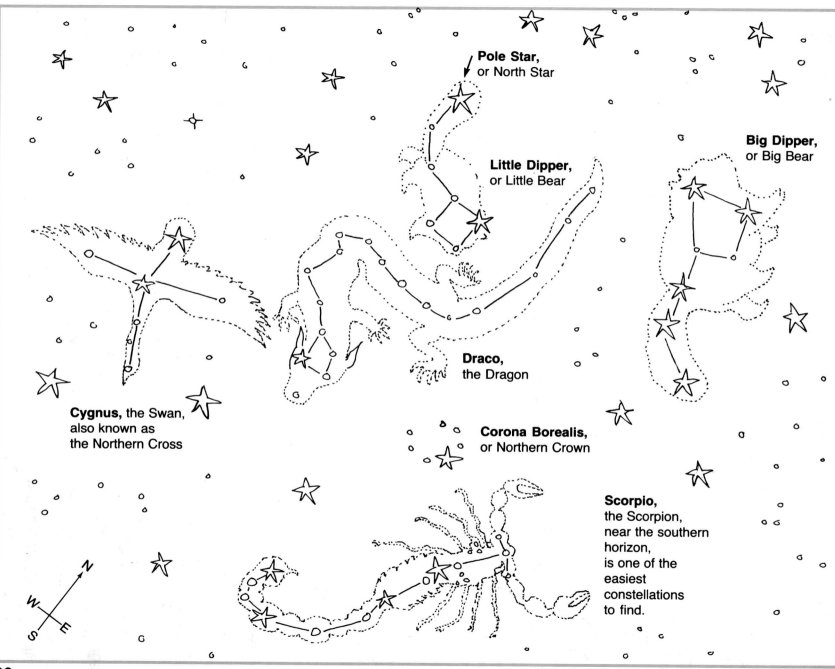

Pole Star, or North Star

Little Dipper, or Little Bear

Big Dipper, or Big Bear

Draco, the Dragon

Cygnus, the Swan, also known as the Northern Cross

Corona Borealis, or Northern Crown

Scorpio, the Scorpion, near the southern horizon, is one of the easiest constellations to find.

N
W   E
S

The Summer Night Sky

On a clear August night, preferably when the moon is not bright, go out and look at the sky. Try to get away from street lights and, if possible, into an open field where trees or buildings will not block your view of the stars.

These are the same starry heavens many ancient people figured time by, sailed ships by, told fortunes by, and spun stories around. The movements of the planets were well understood as far back as 3,000 B.C., especially in China and Egypt.

Ancient people saw patterns and symbolic images in clusters of stars. They called these groupings constellations. Many of the names we use for the constellations, such as Orion, Scorpio, Cassiopeia, and Pegasus, come from Greek and Roman mythology.

Stars consist of great masses of hot gases. They are many times larger than planets, but they look smaller because they are much farther away. There are many good star guides and charts that tell about the night sky.

AUGUST FACTS

■ In England long ago, the name for August was *Weodmonath,* or "the month when weeds flourish."

■ August begins the slowing down of the growing season in nature. Leaves begin drying out on plants and trees; flowers fade; young adult animals leave their family groups. Some birds begin migrating south.

■ The days are shorter, and the sun's path through the sky is already lower toward the horizon.

■ By August's end, there may have been a frost in northern areas.

■ Gardens are full of produce.

■ Trees have prepared most of their buds for next year's growth.

■ The August full moon has been called the Maize Moon by some native American tribes because the corn (maize) is ripe for harvesting.

SEPTEMBER

Preparing for Winter

The shorter hours of daylight and the cooler weather in September are major signals for plants and animals to begin preparing for winter. Many trees and plants disperse their seeds before going into their own winter dormancy. Some plants die completely, some die back to the roots, and some, like deciduous trees, just drop their leaves.

Animals hunt for winter resting places and begin storing food and eating more to add body fat as insulation and reserve energy for the lean months to come. Berries, seeds, fruits, and nuts are fast energy foods for them, and many of these foods store well.

1. The gray squirrel gathers leaves to line its winter nest hole in the tree.

2. The vole collects seeds in its cheeks to store for eating later.

3. The chipmunk digs a winter burrow.

4. Fruits of wild roses are eaten by mice and birds.

5. Many dogwood berries are eaten by birds.

6. Seeds of weeds are food for birds and small animals throughout the fall and winter.

7. On warm, sunny days, a few bumblebees still collect pollen and nectar from late-blooming flowers.

8. The sun now rises more than an hour later and sets 2 hours earlier than it did in June.

9. Woollybear caterpillars find bark crevices or other similar hiding places in which to spend the winter.

Explore your own schoolyard or neighborhood. Look for the activities of fall preparation. Contrast them with what you would see in January or in May. Draw and write about what you see, hear, smell, and touch. Can you find leaves turning color; flowers still in bloom; birds hunting for berries or insects; insects feeding on plants, berries, and fruits; dried seeds and nuts that you can collect?

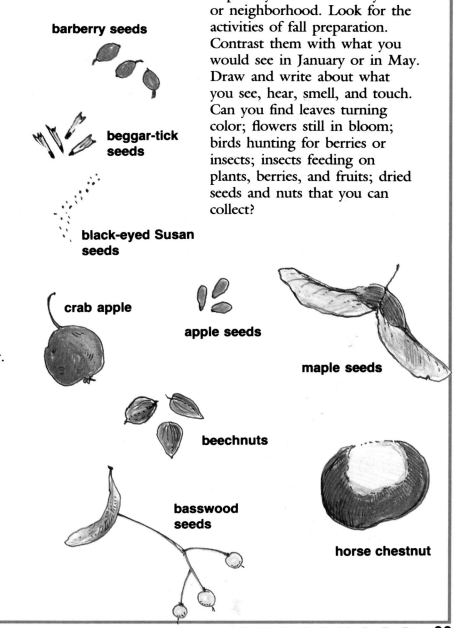

barberry seeds

beggar-tick seeds

black-eyed Susan seeds

crab apple

apple seeds

maple seeds

beechnuts

basswood seeds

horse chestnut

Some Birds That Migrate in the Fall and Spring

SEMIPALMATED SANDPIPER

It belongs to the group of birds called shorebirds that migrate along our East and West coasts.

PEREGRINE FALCON

Watch for hawks and falcons migrating over fields and mountain ranges.

ARCTIC TERN

Each year, it migrates some 11,000 miles from the high Arctic to the Antarctic.

RUBY-THROATED HUMMINGBIRD

It can migrate up to 1,500 miles from its northern range in Canada down to Florida.

CANADA GOOSE

Some will stay north if a winter food supply is plentiful and there is access to open water.

TREE SWALLOW

Along with other swallows, it nests in North America and flies to South America before winter comes.

AMERICAN ROBIN

Some migrate, and some stay year-round where the winter temperatures are warm enough and food is available.

Bird Migration

Bird migration is a mystery that we do not fully understand. Every spring and fall, thousands of birds make a long and often very difficult flight, sometimes traveling from as far south as the tip of South America to the far north of the Arctic, and back again only 4–6 months later.

Birds that migrate appear to require a warmer climate in winter and a colder climate in summer than those that remain in the same place year-round. Some kinds of birds start south as soon as their young can feed for themselves. Other kinds begin to migrate south when days become shorter and the weather turns colder. Often they fly at night, guiding themselves by the moon, the stars, magnetic fields, and other clues. Those that fly by day follow landmarks and the sun.

What birds migrate out of your area, and what birds remain for the winter? Imagine what it would be like to weigh no more than 4 ounces and to make a trip of 3,000 miles every six months, using only your wings!

A good place to watch birds migrate is along a sandy beach, out on a boat, or on top of a mountain or a ridge. On a foggy night, you can sometimes hear small land birds flying low and calling "chirps" to keep together.

Have a field guide along to help you identify the birds.

You can buy binoculars at a nature center, camera shop, or sports store.

Be sure to ask for advice when buying binoculars, as they can differ in quality and price.

The Beginning of Fall

October, with its colorful landscapes and crystal-clear weather, can be a spectacular month to explore outdoors. These are the last busy days for animals before the cold winter settles in. Go outside and listen for the sounds of activity around you—birds calling, squirrels and chipmunks chattering, late summer crickets and bees still chirping and buzzing. What are the smells of fall?

1. Leaves dropping from trees reveal abandoned birds' nests.
2. Raccoons, squirrels, and mice can share a hollow tree as a winter home.
3. Fallen leaves provide important shelter for many small animals and also help make new soil for next year.
4. The chipmunk is gathering last-minute provisions before going into its hole for the winter.
5. Woodchucks are ready to go into their winter dens.
6. This year's caterpillar, produced from summer's eggs laid by an adult cecropia, has spun a cocoon around a plant leaf, inside which it will transform into a pupa for the winter.
7. The male deer now has antlers and is ready to fight other males to win a mate.
8. The woollybear caterpillar has found a winter home in a bark crevice.
9. The spotted salamander and wood frog have found winter shelter under a pile of leaves.

Collect colored leaves. Make collages by gluing arrangements of leaves on cardboard, ironing them between sheets of waxed paper, or sandwiching them between sheets of clear adhesive paper.

Why Do Leaves Change Color?

When days become shorter and temperatures cooler, deciduous trees—those that drop their leaves in the fall—stop sending water out to their leaves. As the leaves dry, the green chlorophyll (the food-making chemical within the leaf's structure) disappears. Some of the bright colors we begin to see are from chemical pigments that were present in the leaves all summer but were masked by the stronger green pigment of the chlorophyll. Other color pigments are created by changes in the leaf chemistry as it dries out. In northern states, these colors are especially bright, because of the more extreme temperature changes and the particular varieties of trees that grow there, such as sugar maples and paper birches, whose leaves contain colorful pigments.

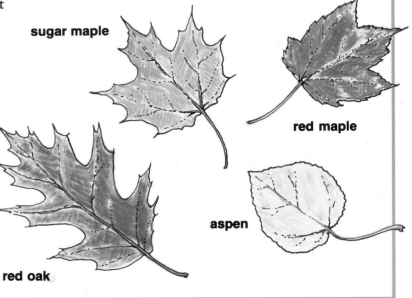

sugar maple

red maple

aspen

red oak

Halloween, a Very Old Fall Festival

Halloween has long been recognized in Europe as both a fall harvest celebration and a religious festival. The name Halloween comes from All Hallow's Eve, the night before All Saints' Day (November 1), when, in some Christian churches, the souls of the dead are prayed for. It became linked with an older, pre-Christian Celtic festival called Samhain that marked the end of summer and of the year. Samhain was a harvest festival and a time when souls of the dead were thought to be nearby. Bonfires, harvest feasting, merrymaking, as well as rituals honoring death and rebirth, took place at this time.

1. Ghost costumes represent the ghosts that were thought to be around on All Hallow's Eve. Trick-or-treating comes from medieval times, when children and poor people begged food at this season to stock up for winter.
2. In pre-Christian communities, witches were considered wise people. They made medicines, told fortunes, gave guidance, did good works, and lived close to nature. Since Samhain was an important harvest celebration for witches, they became associated with Halloween as well.
3. In Europe, historically, a black cat was thought to be a witch in disguise.
4. In early England, squashes were carved out and lit with candles to keep away the increasing darkness and to scare away ghosts.
5. Sheaves of wheat, apples, and squashes are symbols of the fall in Europe. In our country, they have been replaced by corn, apples, and pumpkins.
6. In Western countries, bats are often thought to represent darkness and evil. They are really harmless and fascinating mammals that use their own radar to direct their flight at night.

OCTOBER FACTS

- In many regions, fall leaf color is at its best this month.
- The first hard frost, or even snow, ends the summer garden and sends small animals to their winter homes.
- Most flowers are gone, but the seeds that will produce next year's growth lie under the ground or in drying seed pods.
- Ducks, geese, and hawks head south. Most songbirds that migrate have already gone south.
- The October full moon has been called the Hunter's Moon. Grouse, ducks, geese, deer, bear, moose, and rabbits are hunted now.
- If Standard Time is used, by October 31 the sun is setting almost 2 hours earlier than it did 1 month ago.

A Pond in Late Fall

In November, ponds, lakes, streams, and rivers become places of quiet stillness. Water freezes over, enclosing and protecting a number of animals that sleep through the winter nestled into mud and decaying plant material, or that remain active, but at a slowed pace.

1. Muskrat remain active all winter in their lodges. They will swim out under the ice to forage for underwater vegetation or small snails.
2. Some water turtles dig into mud and sleep, and others remain somewhat active beneath the ice.
3. The red-spotted salamander stays active, but at a slowed pace.
4. Some varieties of frogs burrow into mud and become inactive. (Some frogs winter over in the tadpole stage.)
5. Water snails, beetles, insect larvae, and many other aquatic animals winter over buried in mud or wrapped into submerged plant leaves.
6. Some kinds of fish sleep at the bottom of the pond, while others remain active. (Some fish winter over in the egg stage.)
7. The mallard duck will stay near the pond as long as there is some water. Ducks can swim in cold water and stand on ice because they have thick feather insulation and their feet are specially adapted to keep out the cold.

The Season of Rest

In the cycle of life, many animals and plants need a season of rest and gestation. Even though tree branches appear bare, there are already buds on the twigs. Plants may seem dead, but next summer's growth lies waiting underground in the form of seeds, bulbs, or roots. Even though many insects have died, their young lie resting in egg, larval, or pupal stages. Many animals, such as the beaver and bear, are pregnant in winter, ready to give birth before the first leaves appear on the trees. Choose an animal you would like to know about. Learn what it does during the fall, winter, spring, and summer and report on it to your class.

LIFE CYCLE OF RED-SPOTTED SALAMANDER (NEWT)

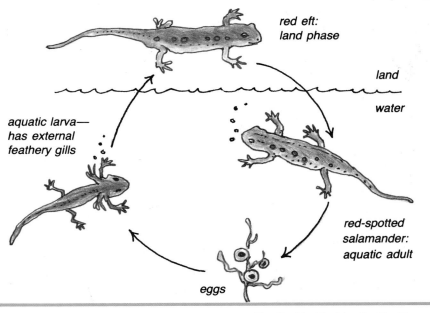

red eft: land phase

land

water

aquatic larva— has external feathery gills

red-spotted salamander: aquatic adult

eggs

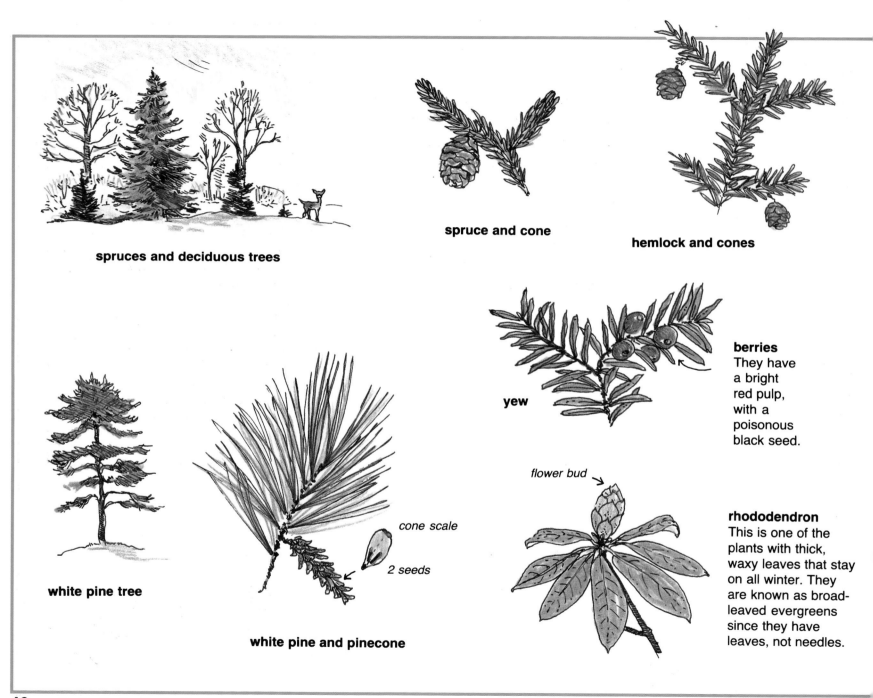

spruces and deciduous trees

spruce and cone

hemlock and cones

berries
They have
a bright
red pulp,
with a
poisonous
black seed.

yew

flower bud

cone scale

2 seeds

white pine tree

white pine and pinecone

rhododendron
This is one of the
plants with thick,
waxy leaves that stay
on all winter. They
are known as broad-
leaved evergreens
since they have
leaves, not needles.

Evergreen Trees

Now the evergreen trees stand out in a landscape no longer brilliant with the leaves of deciduous trees. Why are evergreen trees "evergreen"? If you look closely, you will see that all these trees have needles or scaly leaves that are short and spiked. Needles do not freeze in winter, since the water inside them contains a kind of antifreeze, and they continue to produce enough chlorophyll to stay green. Needles do drop off, but they do so primarily in late spring. Evergreen trees are also called conifers, for they bear cones that house the tree's seeds, 2 inside each scale.

Collect some evergreen branches about 6″ long. Paint 1 side with poster paint or roll on water-based printer's ink. Carefully lay the branch, paint side down, on a piece of paper. Lay another piece of paper or paper towel on top of it. With your fingers or a clean printer's roller, press firmly to create an image of the branch on the paper below. Then carefully remove the branch. Evergreen prints make beautiful cards and decorations.

white pine

hemlock

yew

arborvitae

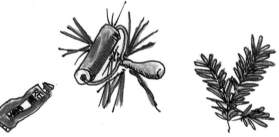

FROST LINE

Winter Begins

It is December, the twelfth month of our calendar. Snow falls, blanketing the world in white and silence. Underneath leaves, rocks, soil, and mud, or inside tree holes, animals sleep away the winter months. Those animals that are still active wait out the storm under dense growth, in rock cavities, or in some other sheltered spot.

1. cecropia moth cocoon
2. woollybear caterpillar
3. bumblebee queen
4. wood frog
5. spotted salamander
6. woodchuck
7. chipmunk
8. earthworm
9. vole (meadow mouse)

hexagonal plate crystal

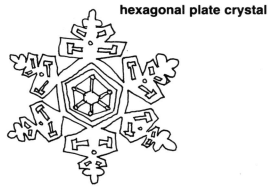

hexagonal plate crystal

needle crystal

Snowflake Shapes

Snowflakes are always hexagonal (6-sided) crystals. But they change shape according to the temperature and where in the air they were formed. In the early 1920s, a Vermont man named W. A. Bentley was able to photograph more than 1,300 individual snowflake designs. Scientists believe there are many more. Look at snowflakes that fall on your sleeve. Can you see the different shapes?

star crystal

granular crystal

MAKE YOUR OWN PAPER SNOWFLAKE

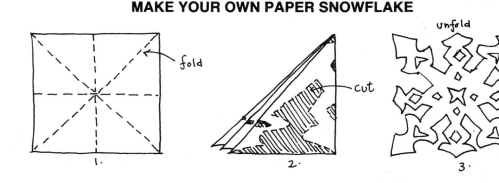

fold

cut

unfold

1.
2.
3.

December Festivals

These are the darkest days of winter. Outdoors, the world of nature is quiet. In pre-Christian Europe, the first day of winter, December 21, was celebrated as a festival to honor light, to keep away the darkness, and to anticipate the sun's return. Bonfires were lit, gifts of food were exchanged, and there was much merrymaking. Over the centuries, many parts of these seasonal celebrations were merged with the early Christian celebrations of Christ's birth, which was thought to have occurred around this same time of year. The Jewish festival Hanukkah and the African harvest festival Kwanzaa are also celebrated in December.

1. The custom of trimming a Christmas tree comes from Germany, where indoor and outdoor trees were decorated at this season.
2. The bright star that supposedly shone over Christ's manger in Bethlehem has long fascinated astronomers. Did it exist? The Wise Men were thought to be astrologers who studied the stars, and the "bright star" they saw and followed may have been an unusual conjunction of the planets Mars, Jupiter, and Saturn.
3. The poinsettia comes from Mexico, where it is called the "flower of the holy night."
4. Holly, ivy, mistletoe, and all winter-green plants were believed by ancient people to have special powers, since winter did not kill them. The ancient Greeks considered the mistletoe a symbol of hope. Enemies would drop their weapons and kiss under it.
5. Fire is an ancient symbol of light conquering darkness, of warmth conquering cold.
6. The lighting of the Hanukkah candles represents the rededication of the holy temple in Jerusalem and the survival of the Jewish nation more than 2,000 years ago.

DECEMBER FACTS

■ This is the last month in our calendar, but in nature there is no beginning or end to the cycle of life.
■ Winter ducks can be seen on ice-free lakes, rivers, and on open salt water.
■ Summer flowers can now be identified by their winter seed heads: goldenrod, milkweed, thistle.
■ The December full moon has been called the Long Night Moon.
■ December 21, the First Day of Winter, begins the first season of our new year. It is the shortest day of the year, when the earth in the Northern Hemisphere is tilted the farthest away from the sun. It is also called the Winter Solstice because this is the time when the sun at midday reaches its lowest position of the year. After this, the sun will gradually raise its path across the sky and the days will lengthen as the earth tilts slowly back toward the sun, heading once more toward summer.

Sunrise—around 7:10 AM.
Sunset—around 4:15 P.M.

(This is Boston time.
Check your area's times.)

Take a walk into a field, wood, or vacant lot. Collect dried seed pods, leaves, pinecones, dried berries, evergreen branches, or sturdy vines. Make a wreath or spray using only natural materials. Add a ribbon and hang on a wall or door.

Bibliography

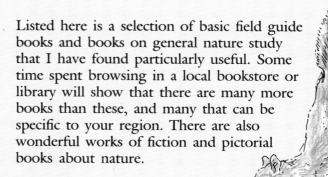

Listed here is a selection of basic field guide books and books on general nature study that I have found particularly useful. Some time spent browsing in a local bookstore or library will show that there are many more books than these, and many that can be specific to your region. There are also wonderful works of fiction and pictorial books about nature.

Field Guides

Burt, William Henry, and Richard Philip Grossenheider. *A Field Guide to Mammals.* Boston: Houghton Mifflin, 1964.

Little, Elbert L., ed. *The Audubon Society Field Guide to North American Trees* (Eastern Region). New York: Alfred A. Knopf, 1980.

Murie, Olaus. *A Field Guide to Animal Tracks,* 2nd ed. Boston: Houghton Mifflin, 1975.

Peterson, Roger Tory, and Margaret McKenny. *A Field Guide to Wildflowers of Northeastern and North-Central North America.* Boston: Houghton Mifflin, 1974.

Robbins, Chandler S., Bertel Bruun, and Herbert S. Zim. *Birds of North America.* New York: Golden Press, 1966.

Scott, Shirley L., ed. *Field Guide to the Birds of North America.* Washington, DC: National Geographic Society, 1983.

Zim, Herbert S. *A Golden Guide: Insects.* New York: Golden Press, 1956. (See also in the Golden Guide series other very useful, inexpensive paperbacks such as *Weeds, Butterflies, Reptiles, Amphibians, Nonflowering Plants, Pond Life, Stars,* and *Weather.*)

General Reference

Allison, Linda. *The Reasons for the Seasons.* Boston: Little, Brown, 1975.

Comstock, Anna B. *Handbook of Nature Study.* Ithaca, New York: Cornell University Press, 1986. (This is a wonderful classic book for children and adults on nature study. It was first published in 1916 by Comstock Publishing Co.)

Durrell, Gerald, and Lee Durrell. *The Amateur Naturalist.* New York: Alfred A. Knopf, 1983.

Hatch, Jane M., ed. *American Book of Days.* New York: H. W. Wilson, 1978. (This gives information about the background of our various national holidays and celebrations.)

Leslie, Clare Walker. *Nature Drawing: A Tool for Learning.* New York: Prentice Hall Press, 1980.

Lingelbach, Jenepher. *Hands-On Nature.* Woodstock, Vermont: Vermont Institute of Natural Science, 1987.

Paton, John, ed. *Nature Encyclopedia.* New York: Checkerboard Press, 1989. (A useful source book written for children as well as adults.)

Rue, Leonard Lee, and William Owen. *Meet the Beaver.* New York: Dodd, Mead, 1986. (Also by the same authors and publisher are *Meet the Moose* 1985, and *Meet the Opossum,* 1983. Leonard Lee Rue is a wildlife biologist and writes many excellent books on animals for children and adults.)

Silver, Donald M. *Life on Earth: Biology Today.* New York: Random House, 1983. (A good beginning biology book.)

Wernert, Susan, ed. *North American Wildlife: An Illustrated Guide to 2,000 Plants and Animals.* Pleasantville, NY: The Reader's Digest Association, 1982.

Resource Centers

National Audubon Society, 950 Third Avenue, New York, NY 10022 (They will give you addresses of local and state chapters of the society. If you join the national chapter, you receive their monthly magazine, *Audubon.*)

National Wildlife Federation, 8925 Leesburg Pike, Vienna, VA 22184 (They publish a bimonthly magazine, *National Wildlife,* as well as *Ranger Rick* and *Your Big Backyard,* which are magazines on nature for children.)

You can also get information from local park services, nature centers, town conservation commissions, as well as the biology departments of schools and colleges in your area. There are probably many resources nearby to help you with your nature study. You might ask your local librarian where to begin.

Index

R